THE ULTIMATE GUIDE TO COACHING QUESTIONS:

200 Questions You Can Ask Clients About Life, Career or Business

KASSANDRA VAUGHN

Copyright © 2019 Kassandra Vaughn

All rights reserved.

ISBN:
ISBN-13: 9-781091-09-8169

DISCLAIMER

All rights reserved. This book may not be reproduced in whole or in part without the written permission from the publisher; nor may any part of this book be reproduced, stored in a retrieval system, or transmitted in any form or by any means, electronic, mechanical, photocopying, recording, or other, without written permission from the publisher.

While all attempts have been made to verify the content provided in this book, neither the author or the publisher assumes any responsibility for errors, omissions, or alternative interpretations of the issues discussed herein.

This book is for entertainment purposes only. The views expressed are those of the author and hers alone. These views should not be taken as expert instruction or commands. The reader is 100% responsible for his or her own actions.

Adherence to all applicable laws and regulations, including international, federal, state, and local governing professional licensing, business practices, advertising, and all other aspects of doing business in the US, Canada, or any other jurisdiction is the sole responsibility of the purchaser or reader.

Neither the author nor the publisher assumes any responsibility or liability whatsoever on the behalf of the purchaser or reader of these materials. Any perceived slight of any individual or organization is absolutely unintentional.

CONTENTS

Disclaimer	i
Introduction	1
Chapter 1: Why I Became a Coach	3
Chapter 2: Coaching Models	6
Chapter 3: The Coaching Journey	15
Chapter 4: Coaching Tools and Techniques	19
Chapter 5: The 200 Coaching Questions	28
Chapter 6: What's Next?	38
Would You Like to Know More?	41

YOUR THREE FREE GIFTS

I so appreciate that you invested in the purchase of this book and that you're taking the time to read it. In the spirit of gratitude, I'd like to offer you three free gifts that are exclusive to my book and blog readers (you won't find this offer anywhere else).

The first free gift is a powerful resource list of **200 Powerful Coaching Questions.** If you're looking for a comprehensive guide to coaching questions you can use with clients, this is it!

To grab your copy of **200 Powerful Coaching Questions**, click here or go to https://tinyurl.com/yncb68ws.

Your next gift is a resource guide that covers the **10 Best Coaching Exercises.** If you're looking for effective coaching exercises to use in life and business coaching, this guide will give you a step-by-step walkthrough of the top 10 coaching exercises to use with a variety of clients.

>>>Tap HERE to download your resource guide<<<
https://tinyurl.com/1es655in

Your third gift is a FREE guide that will help you **build your online coaching business.** If you're ready to build a powerful online coaching business, download this guide and get started.

Download your FREE guide below.

>>>Tap here to grab your resource guide to build your online coaching business<<<
https://tinyurl.com/ymt2z6gj

INTRODUCTION

Everything is a choice.
- Unknown

This book is for every coach who's looking to have, at your fingertips, a massive list of coaching questions that you can make your own. When I first became a coach, one of my biggest challenges was figuring out what questions to ask and when to ask them. With the 200 questions presented in this book, you'll have the ability to help clients dig deeper, design action faster and come to clarity with more purpose than you could've achieved without these questions.

For those of you who are reading this book as someone wanting to work on personal development without a coach, the questions you'll find in this book will help you ask questions that delivery the most clarity. I'm a person who's always asking myself questions. I'm constantly looking for more- more ways to learn, more ways to grow, and many more ways to transform. If you're like me, you'll appreciate the 200 questions that will challenge you to level up your life and become MORE of who you really are.

At the end of the day, everything is a choice. Your life is the summation of all the micro-decisions you're making on a daily basis. If you're looking at your life and you don't like what you see, the fastest way to shift begins with asking the right questions… and the right questions will inevitably lead to the right answers.

Overall, this book will help you understand what a coach is, how coaches work with clients, what the coaching journey looks like for both the coach and the coachee, coaching tools and techniques that you can use as a coach or on yourself, and how to adapt the 200 coaching questions provided to suit your needs.

At the end of the day, this book is about you becoming a better coach… to yourself and others. Let's go…

Thank you for purchasing **The Ultimate Guide to Coaching Questions: 200 Questions You Can Ask Clients About Life, Career or Business.**

Kassandra

CHAPTER 1: WHY I BECAME A COACH

Coaching is the universal language of change and learning.
- Unknown

I've been a coach for over twelve years at this point. I began coaching others at a time when coaching wasn't a common thing outside of sports. In 2007, I knew I wanted to teach people how to choose themselves, how to make self-care and fulfilling their life's calling a priority and I knew that the best way to teach that to those struggling to put themselves first would be in a group coaching format.

So I created a group coaching program called 'Choose You' and started with five people meeting once a week and working in an online platform when we weren't in a coaching session. The experience was as transformational for me as it was for the participants in the program. I watched people grow and develop in ways they never imagined they could. From that experience, I knew that I was more than a teacher. I was a coach and the power of what that means has never left me.

Since 2007, I've ventured into different kinds of coaching, including life coaching, pre-divorce coaching, business coaching, career coaching, and even spent a number of years serving as a life coach for women breadwinners. There's power in becoming a coach who focuses on a specific niche of clients.

As a coach, it's so important to ask yourself, on a consistent basis, "Who's my ideal client? What client population lights me up?" and answer that question with absolute transparency and congruence. When I asked myself those questions, it became very clear that coaching clients who are in the pre-divorce stage of a marriage was not for me. Having gone through two divorces and a very bitter custody battle, every time I coached a pre-divorce client, it was like going through my divorce and custody battle all over again. It was too emotionally charged for me.

When I coached women breadwinners, because I was the breadwinner at that time, it was also hard for me. I could so relate to their struggles but I was coaching someone on issues that hit too close to home and, once again, it was emotionally entangling.

When I sat with myself and asked some powerful questions, I quickly came to the realization of who my ideal client is: aspiring women entrepreneurs who are ready to fire their inner critics, find their inner badass and finally build their businesses... and that's where my coaching focus now sits.

Can that change in the future? Absolutely!

But here's the power of being both open to change and clear about what you want as a coach: I now know what niche is best suited to the calling of my life AND it feels right. I also have gone through this enough times that I can tell when things start to not feel right. At that point, I also know what questions to ask and what level of discovery to do to figure out what my next best step is.

That's the gift of being a coach: You know how to help people move from discovery to designing action to producing results. We do that for ourselves and we do that for our clients.

COACH TRAINING

Over the years, I've heard from a number of aspiring coaches and one of the biggest questions I get is this:

Should I get certified as a coach?

It's a tricky question with an equally tricky answer. I went through the process of getting my ACC coaching certification through ICF so I've done the work and I've gone through the process. In my opinion, did that make me a more knowledgeable coach? Yes. Do I understand how to set a coaching agreement, how to do discovery, how to design action and how to hold clients accountable through specific coaching processes? Yes. Am I a better coach or do I know how to successfully brand, market and sell in my business because of my coaching certification? No.

So here's my take on coaching certifications: Make sure that being a coach is something that you absolutely want to do and can make a living at FIRST. Once you establish both of those things, if you still feel the need to pay $8,000 - $15,000 to get a coaching certification, do so. However, keep in mind that some of the most lucrative coaching businesses are run by coaches who NEVER got a coaching certification. At the heart of any business is your ability to market, brand and sell. It doesn't matter how many credentials you have behind your name. If you can't sell, you won't win in business.

Focus on building a coaching business and learning as much as you can about being a phenomenal coach… and then, once you've secured some clients, are making good money, and have exhausted all the free coach training resources you can find, go to a legitimate coach training program and become certified.

At the end of the day, I became a coach to help people see how powerful they truly are, how much of their entire lives can shift in a short period of time and how all of that depends on the one variable they have total and complete control over: their minds. That, to me, is the epiphany of a lifetime. Once you know that you're the decisive element, nothing can stand in your way. That's the power of being a coach who knows, believes and lives that way. That's the power of being coached by someone who does all of the above. We are powerful beings and coaches help us discover and live the truth of who we really are.

CHAPTER 2: COACHING MODELS

**Champions don't show up to get everything they want.
They show up to give everything they have.
- Unknown**

So often, when people think about working with a coach, they think about sports coaches. They envision a person with a whistle shouting "Get it done! Do more! You can do this! Five more reps! Go! Go! Go!" In fact, when I first started coaching people, one of the statements I'd hear frequently is this: "I'm so glad I have a coach! You'll tell me what to do and I'll get it done. I love the accountability of that!"

And there's some truth behind that statement. When you hire a coach, that person will hold you accountable. Here's where the misinterpretation comes in: Coaches do not direct. In fact, if you're a TRUE coach, you RARELY direct. Coaches are not consultants, mentors, teachers or therapists. It is not a coach's job to dive into the first twenty years of your life and do an archeological dig for all of your early childhood trauma. That's the role of a therapist and should be left up to a therapist.

It's not a coach's job to give you a blueprint for everything you need to do to achieve a specific goal. Coaches do not tell you what to do and how to do it. If that's what you're looking for, consultants and mentors are the more equipped role to handle that. Coaches don't even teach you how to do something. That's the role of a teacher, not a coach.

Now... coaches may factor in skills from the different roles we talked about and position them in the questions they ask but it is never a coach's job to tell you what to do, when to do it, how to do it, the timeline for which to do it or take you back to the age of five to discuss your past trauma and live in that space. None of that is what a coach is meant to do.

Coaching is, by definition, the process of partnering with clients in a powerful, thought-provoking way that brings creativity, insight, and personal development to the client through the discovery, design and follow through on thoughts, beliefs and actions uncovered by the client.

While the coach is there to inspire the client through this process, the coach is not the director of journey. The coach is the guide. The coach is the person who asks open-ended questions that helps the client uncover what's wrong, what the solution is, how to implement the solution and what to do next.

Does a coach hold a client accountable to the goals he or she sets? Yes. But there's a key thing in this: the client sets the goal. The client creates the solution to his or her problem. The coach is there to create the space in which the client can discover the answers within. Coaches firmly believe that within the client are all the answers to all the questions he or she will ever ask. No one outside of the client can provide those answers. So coaches aren't meant to fix a client or tell them what to do. Coaches guide a client through the process of discovery that leads to the solutions and, together, the coach and client design action, create accountability systems and the coach holds the client accountable for follow through on those goals.

At the end of the day coaching can be done on an individual basis or it can be done in a group setting. Coaching can happen face-to-face or virtually in a webinar room. Coaching is about creating the space where one-to-one or one-to-many learning conversations can happen. When a client works with a coach, they do experience better results, increased performance, a higher level of motivation, the ability to self-reflect on a deeper level and improvements in one's ability to make and stick to decisions. In order for those benefits to be experienced, coaching has to be a space where respect, transparency, adaptability, neutrality, confidentiality, congruence, and integrity are found.

When you're working with a great coach, you're working with someone who has an extraordinary ability to listen, ask questions, clarify and give feedback. While the coach helps the client navigate the process, the coachee is the one who sets his or her own goals, strategies and actions. Coaching, more so than any other counseling or mentoring approach, is forward-focused. A coach is focused on where you're going way more than he or she is focused on where you've been or where you're currently stuck.

One of the best coaching questions reflects this idea of being forward-focused:
What's next?

That is the heart of how great coaches guide their clients.

When we drill down even further, there are a variety of coaching models and approaches that a coach can take in working with clients. Most of the coaching models draw from the therapy world for its core principles. If you're a coach who wants to focus your coaching method using a specific model, it's important to understand what models are available and how each model differs from the other.

Let's talk about a few coaching models you can use in your practice with clients.

1. The Grow Model (Behavioral Coaching)
Developed in the 1980s, this coaching model focuses on designing behavior and action that will get a client to his or her goal. When you use the GROW model to coach a client, you start with the coaching conversation by asking the client what he or she would like to focus on for this session. Questions you can use in this step include:
- What do you want to focus on in today's session?
- How would you like to use our time today?
- What would you like to look at in today's session?

Once the focus of the session has been established, a coach would then want to come to agreement on what the client's goal is for the session. The point is to create a specific outcome that the client wants to achieve by the end of the session. A question that I like to use to get to this result is "By the end of this session, what would you like to accomplish?"

From there, a coach will use open-ended questions to help a coachee gain clarity, uncover limiting beliefs and explore the root causes of the problem. Questions that bring clarity and awareness include the following:
- What's missing?
- What would you change about this situation?

- What's keeping you up at night?
- Where's your greatest opportunity for change?
- What about this situation is the biggest issue for you?
- What or who's at the source of your frustration?

From there, the coach moves from investigating the problem to developing options or solutions to deal with the problem. This is the place where coaches help the client design action. Coaching questions that would help design action include:
- What's your next step?
- What could change the situation?
- What are your options?
- How would you like to see this play out?
- What's the outcome that you're hoping for?
- How do you get to that outcome?
- What does success look like for you?
- How do you get there from here?

The GROW model wraps with the coach confirming the client's action plan for moving forward, the client's specific next steps, and the timeline for completing those steps. The coach also goes over how accountability will be done between now and the next coaching session. The entire focus of the GROW coaching model is on designing and changing behavior.

2. Solution-Focused Coaching

While solution-focused coaching has its foundation in Milton H. Erickson's approach to strategic therapy, a lot of the solution-focused coaching approach stems from the work of therapists Insoo Kim Berg and Steve de Shazer who created brief solution focused therapy in 1988. Solution-focused therapy believes that focusing on problems is not the answer; focusing on building solutions is. It is a framework of therapy that uses a non-pathological framework. The belief is that the client is the expert in his or her own life rather than the coach. In this way, when we talk about solution-focused coaching, it centers around the client being resourceful enough to take action that produces positive change.

When a coach uses solution-focused coaching, the focus is on the future. A solution-focused coach is all about helping the client disengage from the problem and spend the bulk of his or her time focusing on creating solutions. A coach using this model would also focus on resource activation. In this way, the coach would help the client see how many resources (both internal and external) he or she has access to.

When it comes to solution-focused coaching, one of my favorite questions to ask is the miracle question. This question invites the client to imagine and describe in detail how the future would be different when the problem no longer exists. Here's the miracle question:

I am going to ask you a rather strange question [pause]. The strange question is this: [pause] After we talk, you go back to your work (home, school) and you do whatever you need to do the rest of today, such as taking care of the children, cooking dinner, watching TV, giving the children a bath, and so on. Then it's time to go to bed. Everyone in your house is quiet, and you're sleeping in peace. In the middle of the night, a miracle happens and the problem that prompted you to talk to me today is solved! But because this happened while you were sleeping, you have no way of knowing that there was an overnight miracle that solved the problem. [pause] So, when you wake up tomorrow morning, what might be the small change that will make you say to yourself, 'Wow, something must have happened—the problem is gone!"

Once the coach thoroughly explores the miracle, he or she would then ask "On a scale of 0 to 10 with 0 being the worst things have ever been and 10 being the miracle day, where are you now? Where would things need to be for you to know that you didn't need to see me anymore? What will be the first things that will let you know you are 1 point higher?"

The miracle question, in this way, becomes a series of questions that helps the client explore what living the miracle would be like.

Other ways to ask the miracle question include:

> If you woke up tomorrow, and a miracle happened so that you no longer allowed others to walk all over you, what would you see differently?
> What would the first signs be that the miracle occurred?

The power of being a solution-focused coach is that you keep the client focused on creating solutions rather than getting stuck in the problem. It's pretty miraculous when you know how to use this model well.

3. Cognitive Behavioral Coaching

CBC derives from the therapy world as well. It stems from the work of Aaron Beck (1976) and Albert Ellis (1962). The focus of CBC is to help clients examine and change thoughts and beliefs. A coach who uses Cognitive Behavioral Coaching would start by asking a client to talk about his or her problems or concerns. The coach would then help the client establish specific, measurable goals that the client is capable of achieving. Throughout the coaching session, the coach would help the client develop actions plans, next steps and determine how accountability will be maintained between this and the next coaching session. At the core of CBC is the idea that thoughts creating feelings, feelings create behavior and behavior reinforces thoughts. For any coach who likes to help clients develop new habits, this is a powerful coaching model to use.

4. NLP Coaching

NLP coaching is based on Neurolinguistic Programming. At the heart of NLP is the idea that getting into the right state is critical to changing behavior. For a client to be successful in achieving his or her goals, he or she needs to be able to access the right states (emotional and physical) to support the goals being achieved. NLP coaching is firmly grounded in uncovering and shifting the largely unconscious sorting patterns that we use to perceive and respond to life experiences.

Examples of NLP coaching questions include:
> What are you doing now to achieve your end goal?
> What are you doing now to sabotage yourself in achieving your end goal?

- ➤ What feedback have you received from your stakeholders on where you are now?
- ➤ What are the positive things that result from this behavior?
- ➤ What else do you get out of this choice? What are all of the benefits?
- ➤ Which of these benefits do you know you want to keep? Or, what are the benefits you simply can't live without?
- ➤ In what other ways can you meet each identified positive need?

From an NLP coaching perspective, once you can get a client to understand how to move into the best states of being, you can help the client take action from those states which then allows them to change behavior and transform his or her life.

5. Transpersonal Coaching

Transpersonal coaching is a model of coaching that has its foundation in transpersonal psychology. Transpersonal coaching coaches the whole person. It incorporates seven interconnected levels upon which we experience ourselves. These seven levels include:

1. Body
2. Mind
3. Emotion
4. Shadow
5. Connection
6. Soul
7. Spirit

Transpersonal means that it goes beyond the personal and includes universal elements such as spirituality and the human psyche. In this way, the transpersonal approach to coaching takes a system approach. There's a firm belief in this coaching model that we're all interconnected. What one person accomplishes impacts all others. The yearning that people have is beyond the material world. More than anything else, transpersonal coaching focuses on the fact that personal and spiritual development aren't separate things. It isn't a one and done process but a lifelong evolution that we all go through together.

To use a transpersonal coaching approach, you have to really believe in the mind-body-spirit connection inherent in all people. The transpersonal focuses on meaning, purpose and direction. In this way, a coach invites his or her client to reframe life as an evolutionary process. This is a coach approach that recognizes the power each person has to both create and destroy. For a transpersonal coach, the goal is to empower the client to reframe limiting beliefs so he or she can reach his or her true potential.

6 Appreciative Coaching

I ascribe to the appreciative coaching approach. I love it because it incorporates so much of the other coaching models but has its own distinct framework. The Appreciative Coaching approach is based on the Appreciative Inquiry (AI) model of growth. In AI, there are four stages: discovery, dream, design and destiny. As an appreciative coach, one believes that our goal, in working with clients, is to partner with them in a positive, generative approach where the client is the agent of his or her own change.

In the four-stage process, discovery is the first stage and is about helping the client reflect and discover his or her strengths and abilities. The second stage, dream, is all about helping the client envision and articulate the future that the client desires. The third stage is design. This is where the coach and client craft strategies that will get them to the fourth stage: destiny. The fourth stage is destiny. The destiny stage is about seeing and living the dream in the present.

Examples of appreciative coaching questions include:
- Describe your three greatest accomplishments to date
- What made those accomplishments stand out for you?
- Tell me what worked in the past
- Thinking about your dream, what would make it come alive for you?
- What three big accomplishments would make you feel as though you have come close to your dream?
- What are times when you feel at your best?
- What gives you energy?
- What are the possibilities?

- What is the world calling you to be?
- What is the gift in this challenge?
- What opportunities are you not taking advantage of?
- What do you really, really want?

There are many more coaching models than the ones I've described in this chapter. If you're a coach who wants to follow a specific model, read about all of them. Build mastery in the coaching model that most aligns with your core beliefs, values and vision for coaching. Practice that specific coaching model on every coaching call. Eventually, practicing a specific model of coaching will become as natural to you as breathing. It takes time and the benefits will be worth it.

CHAPTER 3: THE COACHING JOURNEY

**What you get by achieving your goals is not as important as
what you become by achieving your goals.
- Zig Ziglar**

Coaching others to greatness is one of the most fulfilling professions you can take on. It's a gift to be a part of a process where you begin working with someone at one level of life and, over time, watch them grow, shift and evolve to an entirely different level of living. Most people have no idea of how much they can transform and grow. As a coach, you get to witness this process over and over again.

For most people who choose to become coaches, this is what draws them in. Being an instrumental part of life transformation is intoxicating and immensely satisfying. However, that's not the only part of the coaching experience and while it's important to know the WHY behind becoming a coach, it's also important to understand and honor the valleys that exist along your coaching journey.

As a coach (especially as a new coach), there will be clients you take on that are for you and clients you take on that are NOT your clients. The clients that are for you align with your core values, the way you work, the coaching relationship and are ready to commit and deliver upon the expectations of the coaching dynamic. The clients that are NOT for you might pay the money and they might say that they're ready to do the work but, along the way, you quickly discover that they're more invested in telling a victim story than they are in doing the work of changing their lives. Before you know it, you become a frustrated coach because you now realize you've taken on a client who is, at this moment, uncoachable. This happens alot.

It's important to recognize that your moments of dissatisfaction with clients that are not for you is not your entire coaching business. More than that, it's important to use those moments of frustration to shift how you vet and take on clients so you ONLY take on clients that are your ideal. At first, it will feel highly selective and maybe even a little snobbish to turn people away. After all, so many people 'need' you, right? Wrong! When you take on clients who aren't meant for you, it becomes a struggle for both you and that client. In addition to that, when you accept money from a client you know will be a pain, you are treating your talents and gifts as if they can be sold to the highest bidder. That is not the way you want to show up in the world.

At the end of the day, what fulfills you as a coach is your ability to help people change their lives. When you take on clients who might pay but won't do the work, you waste your talent and time on clients who will not help you fulfill your mission in the world. No matter how you slice it, if a client isn't ready to do the work, they won't... and you are not answering the calling on your life if you're wasting your time on those clients. Learn how to selectively screen and select your clients. Yes, you will say No to money that you could easily need and, yes, you'll grow your coaching business much faster by not taking on clients who are not in alignment with you. Learn the lesson before you have to pay the consequences of not heeding it.

At the same time that the coaching journey is about helping others transform their lives, the coaching journey is also about you evolving as a person, a coach, and a spiritual being... and, so often, aspiring coaches will halt the process of officially becoming a coach because they don't feel 'ready.' In other words, a coach will look at her life and say "My life's a mess. How could I possibly help someone else?" or "I'm going to wait until life calms down and then I'll pursue becoming a coach" or "I'm not successful. How can I coach anyone on anything?" So many coaches keep their light hid under a bushel out of fear that they aren't good enough, successful enough, smart enough or experienced enough to be a coach.

Here's the deal: The best coaches are authentic. They own their shit and live their truth openly and unapologetically. An authentic coach is a coach who's REAL- real about the challenges of life, real about his or her limitations, real about the fact that growth is messy and real about the fact that she has struggles like all of her clients do... and you can't be an authentic coach if you're spending all of your time trying to be the perfect coach with the perfect life. Remember: facades don't create transformation; real life does.

There is no perfect time to become a coach. You might have your entire life together- perfect relationship, perfect home life, perfect family, become a coach and, within three months of doing so, have your entire life fall apart. You cannot predict the circumstances of your life. What you can do is be the most present, available for the journey, aligned with your purpose, and connected to resilience coach that you can be. That is what will attract your best clients and an amazing business and that is also what will hold down the stability of your coaching business when the going gets really rough. Until you learn how to thrive in the storm, you will always be crushed by it. Becoming a coach has nothing to do with being perfect and everything to do with honoring your value given the fact that you're not.

At the end of the day, the journey to becoming a coach is about who you're becoming in the process of your life. You don't have to look at it like it's some resume of credentials that you 'must' have before you can enter the arena. The best coaches coach from their hearts, their spirits and their life experiences. Yes, they may have a coaching credential but that's not the reason that transformation happens. Transformation happens because the coach is fully present, the client is aligned and the experience is treated with the level of honor and sacred attention that it deserves. Only then can you be a powerful coach… and being present has nothing to do with being perfect. In fact, the more you strive to be perfect, the more ground you lose in being present.

Your coaching journey is as much about who you become along the way as it is about who your clients become as a result of working with you. It's a powerful experience for all involved. Don't shortchange the process by wasting years to become someone you were never meant to be. In the coaching relationship, you are both student and teacher… and your clients (the ones who are truly for you) have a lot to teach you right now. Don't delay your learning journey by waiting to 'feel' ready. If what you want is a list of credentials, you'll always find a new one to get. If what you crave is a life of meaning and work that impacts the world, you're ready to start that today.

Don't delay. Be the coach you are right now because who you are, right now, is enough.

CHAPTER 4: COACHING TOOLS AND TECHNIQUES

Discomfort is the currency of success.
- Brooke Castillo

As a coach, there are so many tools and techniques you can use to help clients transform their lives. In this chapter, let's talk about five coaching tools and three coaching techniques.

Here are the five coaching tools we'll cover:
1. The coaching agreement
2. Powerful questions
3. Silence
4. Accountability measures
5. Coaching recaps

Here are the three coaching techniques we'll cover:
1. 1:1 coaching
2. Group coaching
3. E-coaching

COACHING TOOL #1: THE COACHING AGREEMENT

At the foundation of every coaching conversation is the coaching agreement. The coaching agreement is the process by which a coach and client set the terms of what will be focused on, discussed and achieved on any given coaching call. The coaching agreement is one of the first things a coach learns when participating in a formal coach training program.

What's in the coaching agreement?

When done by the book, the coaching agreement involves the following steps:

Step 1: Greet the client and establish rapport.
When you first meet a client or get on a phone call with a client, you begin with a welcome and establishing rapport. They key is to get an idea of how

the client is feeling, what's been going on in the client's life between the last session and the current one and setting the tone for what's going to happen during today's session.

How long should Step 1 take? One to three minutes.

Step 2: Set the coaching agreement.
After rapport has been established, the coaching agreement will be set. What's the coaching agreement? It's a question that lays out the purpose and goals of the current session. The coaching agreement can be set using a question such as "By the end of this call, what would you like to have accomplished?" or "By the end of our call today, what would you like to walk away with?" The goal is to have the client tell the coach what he or she wants to get accomplished by the end of this coaching session.

How long should Step 2 take? Three to five minutes.

Step 3: Explore the issues.
Steps 3 and 4 are the longest part of the coaching call. In Step 3, the coach spends a great deal of time asking open-ended questions to explore the key issues that are impacting what the client would like to achieve. In this step, a coach might explore limiting beliefs, past experiences, current self-doubts and ways in which the client is self-sabotaging the process.

How long should Step 3 take? Ten to fifteen minutes.

Step 4: Design action.
In step 4, the coach moves from exploring the issue to designing action to move forward on the client's goal. This is the strategic part of the coaching session. In this step, open-ended questions will be focused on developing strategies and taking action that will achieve the client's stated goals.

How long should Step 4 take? Fifteen to twenty minutes.

Step 5: Create accountability measures.
Once an action plan has been designed, it's time to decide how accountability will be established and maintained. In this step, the coach

will ask the client how he or she wants to be held accountable. Together, they'll decide how communication will be maintained between coaching sessions, what the client will do to communicate that goals have been met and how the coach will respond should goals not be met.

How long should Step 5 take? Two to four minutes.

Step 6: Evaluate session outcomes.
At this point in the session, the coach comes back to the original goals the client indicated that he or she wanted to achieve by the end of the session. The coach discusses whether or not the client's session goals were achieved.

How long should Step 6 take? Two to four minutes.

Step 7: Recap next steps, schedule the next appointment and end the call.
The coach asks the client to recap what his or her next steps will be. It's important for the client to articulate what his or her next action steps are as well as the way in which accountability will be maintained.

How long should Step 7 take? Three to four minutes.

Step 8: Email a coaching recap.
Once you end the call, compile the notes from the session, put it in a coaching recap, and email the client the coaching recap. Coaching recaps can also be placed on a secure private website that is for the client's eyes only. The coaching recap gives the client documentation that spells out how the session went and the level to which the client has progressed.

How long should Step 8 take? Ten to thirty minutes after the coaching call.

COACHING TOOL #2: POWERFUL QUESTIONS
At the heart of coaching is the use of powerful, open-ended questions. While you will find 200 of those coaching questions in Chapter 5, let's talk about why powerful questions matter. Most people rarely ask themselves powerful questions. In fact, during the average day, most people are asking

themselves and others close-ended powerless questions. Even when people ask each other open-ended questions like "How are you?", in many instances, they're not present enough or interested enough to listen to the answer.

As a coach, the questions you ask will help your client move in the direction needed. Knowing what questions to ask and how to ask them becomes incredibly important. In this way, it's important to craft powerful questions that feel right when you say them, that deliver the message you intend and that create the space for your clients to do some discovery. Very often, those questions will be in short form. For example, if I wanted to understand a client's limiting beliefs and how those beliefs are keeping a client stuck, I could ask any of the following:

- What limiting belief is holding you back the most?
- How are your limiting beliefs getting in the way of achieving your dream?
- When you think about why this dream won't happen, what reasons are you telling yourself?

All three questions are powerful and open-ended. However, when we ask really long coaching questions, clients can get stuck on certain words or not understand what we're asking for. In most situations, concise, direct, powerful coaching questions work a lot better.

If I wanted to get at a client's limiting beliefs by using shorter coaching questions, I could ask any of the following:
- What's getting in the way?
- What's holding you back?
- What's missing in your strategy?
- What's keeping you from moving forward?
- What beliefs aren't serving you?
- How is that belief hurting your ability to take action?
- What's your level of self-belief?
- Where's your self-doubt coming from?

Any of those questions will dive into a client's limiting beliefs and help the client get to the heart of the issue. The best way to get good at creating and using powerful questions is to practice using them often (both in your home life and in your professional life). Whenever you can ask an open-ended, powerful question, ask one and see what happens.

At the end of the day, powerful questions remind clients that they have the ability to change. It empowers them to take action. It creates buy-in for the coaching process. Clients are usually more capable than they give themselves credit for. Powerful questions can stimulate people to access their own brilliance and come up with their own solutions. When people feel a sense of ownership for the solutions and action steps that arise from the coaching conversation, they become more motivated to take those actions. When you ask a client powerful questions, it gives the client the opportunity to uncover what the client really wants, what's most important, and how to bring the most satisfaction and fulfillment to life.

The art of asking powerful questions comes from knowing the right direction to take them (where), having the right intentions (why), using the right questions (what) and (which), asking them in the right way (how), asking them about the right person (who), and asking at the right time (when). To ask powerful questions, you have to be curious and courageous on the client's behalf. You need to believe that the client is able to handle tough, direct questions. You have to trust your ability to use the right question at the right moment. You also have to be on the lookout for teachable moments when inserting a direct question will energize change.

COACHING TOOL #3: SILENCE

Silence is a powerful coaching skill to develop… and most people don't like long pauses in conversation. Think about it. Can you, in a conversation, be silent for thirty seconds? In other words, can you hold a conversation with someone, ask them a question and allow for thirty seconds where you don't move, don't nod, don't say "Hmm" or "Uh huh", and remain absolutely silent? Most people can't do that. In fact, when you first practice it, because most people are used to being interrupted by others, the other person will actually stop mid-sentence and say "Are you listening?" and, yet, silence offers clients the space to do some meta-cognition (think about what they're thinking about) and actually go deeper for the answers within.

Silence, in the coaching sense, is a phenomenal tool. It allows the client to think through their problems, to go deeper into the core of what's at issue, and to listen to their intuition and retrieve the answers only the client has. Far too often, inexperienced coaches fill coaching calls with tons of questions and reframed statements but don't allow enough space and time for silence. If you want to get to the bottom of why a client is doing what he or she is doing or how to change something in a client's life, practice silence and notice how easily and how quickly the client retrieves the answers.

How do you develop coaching skill in silence?

Practice asking friends, family and clients a powerful, open-ended question about something that's concerning them and then doing 30 seconds of silence. You can either time your 30 seconds with a watch that you glance at periodically or count time the old-fashioned way in your head (one Mississippi, two Mississippi, three Mississippi). The more you practice silence, the less uncomfortable it will feel and the better at it you'll become.

COACHING TOOL #4: ACCOUNTABILITY MEASURES

Holding clients accountable for the actions they committed to taking is a key responsibility of any coach. It's one thing to brainstorm and design action. It's another thing to follow through and take the action. In this way, accountability measures (or how you hold clients accountable) is critical to coaching success... and accountability won't always feel comfortable. There will be times when you have to get real with a client and troubleshoot why they aren't following through on the commitments they made and the conversation can be filled with tension and resistance. As a coach, you need to be ready for that. As a coach, you need to prepare your clients in advance for those kinds of conversations.

When we talk about accountability measures, there are a number of things you can do to create accountability with clients. Here are some strategies to use:

1. Ask clients how they would like to be held accountable.
2. In your intro conversation with a client, explain how you hold clients accountable and what your definition of accountability is.
3. By the end of each call, agree to the method, timing and way in which the client will let you know his or her level of progress.
4. Develop a measuring system that both you and the client can see to evaluate, on a weekly basis, what percentage of the goals the client reaches. The visual display of achievement (or lack thereof) is a powerful demonstration of what is or isn't working.
5. Do text check-ins on a daily basis to help the client stay focused on the daily decisions that need to be made to meet the weekly goals.
6. Work backwards on a client's goals. In other words, set up 90-day goals, 60 day goals, 30 day goals and 7 day goals. With that framework set up, it's very clear what the client needs to focus on this week without overwhelming the client with what needs to get done in three months.

At the end of the day, the point of accountability is to measure how consistently the client does what he or she says he or she is going to do. In the accountability framework, excuses, the blame game, and 'valid reasons' don't matter. Either the client is keeping the commitment she makes to herself or she's not and the results will be the deciding factor of a client's success in following through on goals.

COACHING TOOL #5: COACHING RECAPS

During a coaching session, it's important to take ample notes. Be sure to include key questions that were asked, the client's responses, and any changes in emotion, decision or clarity. Once the session has ended, create a system for recording and saving your notes. From there, email the client a coaching recap (preferably the same day).

The power of coaching recaps cannot be understated. My clients love having a historical record of their transformation and growth. They typically print out the coaching recaps, save them in a binder, and review them regularly. Yes, creating coaching recaps takes a solid amount of time (anywhere from ten minutes to thirty minutes if you recorded notes during the session by hand) but it's definitely worth the time spent.

Now that we've covered coaching tools, let's discuss three coaching techniques you can use with clients.

COACHING TECHNIQUE 1: One-to-one coaching

One-to-one coaching is a powerful method of coaching. In this technique, the coach works with one client. This technique of coaching can happen in person, via telephone, and virtually using a webinar room, Skype, Facetime or another method of video conferencing. The benefits of one-to-one coaching is that it offers a greater level of focus and clarity for the client. It also allows you to build trust, confidence and accountability in a shorter period of time. When done in a face-to-face setting, it's even more powerful. Being able to see a person's body language and connect in the same space cannot be underscored.

From a business perspective, the challenge with one-to-one coaching is that it's not scaleable. There are 24 hours in a day and 7 days in a week. If your entire coaching business is based on one-to-one coaching, you will have a ceiling on the amount of money you're making every year and that ceiling will still exist even when you hire additional coaches to cover new clients. At some point, if you have a coaching practice that you want to take beyond low six figures, you'll need to implement more scaleable coaching techniques.

COACHING TECHNIQUE 2: Group coaching

Group coaching is the process of coaching more than one person at a time. In a solid business model, group coaching represents a coaching structure where you register a cohort of clients (5 to 25 or more people) and work with that cohort for a number of weeks. The coach meets with the group on a weekly basis for anywhere from thirty minutes to two hours. During the live coaching session, the coach can do any number of things, including round robbin or laser coaching, hot seat coaching for one or two members of the group while others take notes and provide feedback, or part training/part coaching on a specific coaching topic for that week.

It is critical that trust and synergy are developed early in the group coaching process. To do this, a coach needs to be selective on who applies and is admitted into a group coaching program. It only takes one person to ruin the group coaching experience so ensuring that people of like mind are brought together for a unified purpose is key.

COACHING TECHNIQUE 3: E-coaching

E-coaching is usually an add-on to one-to-one or group coaching. Whether done via email, text or private message, e-coaching gives the client (or clients) the opportunity check in with the coach, to troubleshoot in-the-moment challenges, and to refocus on what really matters. Because e-coaching can create the opportunity for 24/7 access to a coach, it's really important to specify (in writing) the extent to which a client will have access to the coach via e-coaching. In addition, be clear on the turnaround time for a response to a message. All of this will help to keep the coach's work/life harmony intact.

The beauty of coaching is that you have so much freedom to decide who you coach, how you coach, and the techniques you use with each client. While there will be uncomfortable moments in coaching and there will be times when clients are resistant to change, you have the ability to create sacred space, a nurturing environment and the level of challenge and opportunity necessary to help clients move to the next levels of their lives. Feel the gratitude of what you have the privilege of doing and create a coaching practice that reflects all of who you are, what you love, and what you were put on the earth to do.

CHAPTER 5: THE 200 COACHING QUESTIONS

**We tend to forget that baby steps still move you forward.
- Unknown**

Powerful questions are the heart and soul of coaching. There are so many books that will teach you how to coach, how to set up a coaching business, and how to find and get coaching clients. Very few books give you an exhaustive list of coaching questions... and here's why that's vital to your success: the ability to ask powerful questions is what will get your clients results. The better results you get for clients, the more clients you'll have.

And here's the thing: unless you have a repository of powerful questions to ask, you'll get into the bad habit of constantly asking the same questions. For example, how many times have you asked one of the below questions?

- What's your goal?
- What would your next steps be?
- How have things gone?
- What's the update?
- Where are you struggling?
- How can you set yourself up for success?
- What are the possibilities?
- What's next?
- What would that look like?
- What is your biggest challenge?
- What needs to change?

Now... all of the above questions are solid coaching questions to ask. But when you consistently ask the same questions, the impact of each question is lessened... which is why having a large repository of questions to choose from is important.

The 200 questions below fall under different coaching categories: general coaching, life coaching, business coaching and career coaching. Many of the questions can fit into all of the coaching categories. As you read through the questions, jot down the questions that feel right to you. Feel free to change the wording of the question so it sounds like something you'd say. Most importantly, practice the questions on every person you can. The more you practice, the better you'll become at asking questions.

One thing to keep in mind: the more powerful the question, the more likely a client is to feel stumped by the question, to respond with "I don't know" or to feel overwhelmed by the level of depth the client is being asked to go into. As a coach, it can be very frustrating to ask a powerful question and receive a response that says, "Umm, I don't know…"

So what do you do when that happens?

There are a number of approaches you could take. When a client is stumped by a question, you've asked, you can follow up with any one of the following questions:
- If you did know, what would your answer be?
- If you had an adult child who was going through the same exact thing, what advice would you give your child?
- You may not have the answer but if you were to move in the direction of the answer, what would you do next?

No matter what, don't give up when a client says "I don't know" or goes silent. Continue asking questions until clarity arrives.

USING THE 200 QUESTIONS
Below are 200 coaching questions. They fall into one of four brackets:
1. *General coaching questions*

    General coaching questions can be used in all coaching situations. Some of the questions relate to starting the coaching conversation. Other questions are designed to help the client explore and design action. These are questions you can use in a variety of settings.

2. *Life coaching questions*

    Life coaching questions can be used when the purpose of the coaching relationship is to help the client work on key life goals. Examples of these goals include losing weight, changing careers, strengthening relationships, or pursuing personal development interests that require stepping out of comfort zones. Many life coaching questions are used when doing career or business coaching because life and business/career are inseparable.

3. *Business coaching questions*

Business coaching questions focus on building, growing and sustaining a business. These questions can be used with aspiring entrepreneurs who haven't started a business. They also work for new and established entrepreneurs. The goal of business coaching is to help clients create and grow successful businesses which requires looking at the vision of the business as well as the methods and means of generating revenue in that business.

4. *Career coaching questions*

Career coaching questions are designed to help clients get clarity about career options, decisions, and the best approach to take to shift, change or elevate a career. The questions center around determining specific career development goals and the strategies by which to achieve them.

General Coaching Questions

1. What would you like to focus on today?
2. How could we best use our time today?
3. What's the topic for our coaching conversation?
4. What did you learn from this?
5. What would you do differently next time?
6. When was the last time you were out of your comfort zone and how did that make you feel?
7. What challenges are you struggling with at the moment?
8. What's the worst thing that can happen if you try and fail?
9. On a scale of 1 - 10 how confident are you of achieving this goal?
10. What's stopping you from achieving this goal?
11. What does your intuition tell you about this goal?
12. If you were advising someone else on how to achieve this, what would you tell them to do?
13. What's the one thing that will stop this from being successful?
14. What activities do you do where you feel like you just go "into the zone", and you totally lose track of time?
15. What would you do if you had unlimited resources?

16. If you did know the answer, what would it be?
17. What am I not asking you that you really want me to ask?
18. What are you afraid of?
19. What are you passionate about?
20. What is the biggest obstacle that you are facing?
21. Where are you sabotaging yourself?
22. What do you think you should do first?
23. What would be the most helpful thing you could do now?
24. If you were guaranteed to succeed, what would you do?
25. If you could only do one thing this week, what would it be?
26. What books should you be reading to help you achieve your goals?
27. What are you going to do in the next 24 hours?
28. Who do you need to speak to about this goal?
29. How are you going to celebrate reaching your goal?
30. What have you tried so far?
31. How have you handled something like this before?
32. What was the outcome?
33. What's the first thing you need to do to resolve this?
34. What opportunities do you have right now?
35. What energizes you? What drains you?
36. What would you like to discuss now?
37. What was most valuable for you in our discussion?
38. What are you grateful for?
39. Who's grateful for you?
40. How would you like it to be?
41. What does this mean to you?
42. What's the benefit of this problem?
43. Which step could you take that would make the biggest difference right now?
44. What are you willing to do to improve this situation?
45. Who did you have to become to achieve it?
46. How will you transform your life with this new knowledge?
47. What did you learn?
48. What is your top priority right now?
49. What are the possibilities?
50. If you had your choice, what would you do?
51. What do you think?
52. How does it look to you?
53. How do you feel about it?
54. What seems to confuse you?
55. What happened?
56. Then what?
57. What is the part that is not yet clear?

58. What resonates for you?
59. What are the chances of success?
60. What options can you create?
61. What will that get you?
62. Where will this lead?
63. What is the opportunity here?
64. What is the challenge?
65. What is your assessment?
66. How is this working?
67. What are the benefits and downside of each option?
68. So what will you do now and when?
69. And how will you overcome it?
70. How likely is the option to succeed?
71. What situations tend to bring out your best?
72. What are you learning and accepting about yourself at present?
73. Tell me what worked in the past.
74. How can you help yourself?
75. How did you discover that?
76. How would you say that differently?
77. What have you already started putting in place?
78. How will you know?
79. How have you explored what you're capable of?
80. What if there were no limits?
81. What is motivating you?
82. What are you willing to do to make this work?
83. What opportunities are you not taking advantage of?
84. What are you willing to commit to this week that would give you a sense of accomplishment?
85. What behavior or assumptions do you need to give up or abandon in order to achieve your goal? This holds true in thinking as well as strategy, action and habit. Sometimes in order to grow, you have to let go.
86. What's the biggest change you are willing to make this week, starting today?
87. What are the three measurable activities you can commit to this week and the outcomes you expect that will move you closer to your goal?
88. What change in your thinking would help you achieve your goals faster and in a more enjoyable way?
89. What can you do in the next week to make you happier and more purposeful?
90. What do you want to accomplish in the next year?

Life Coaching Questions

91. Looking into the future, who are you called to be? What work are you called to do?
92. What do you notice about yourself when you dream of your future?
93. If you could communicate with yourself in the future, what questions would you want to ask yourself? What would you like others to ask of you?
94. How does the dream fit into the vision you have for your life?
95. What is the world calling you to be?
96. What is the inspiration of your life?
97. Who would you have to become to have all that you want?
98. Thinking about your dream, what would make it come alive for you?
99. What in your dream really calls to you, makes you year for its fulfillment?
100. When you think about your dream, what brings you joy or excitement? What makes you laugh?
101. What three big accomplishments would make you feel as though you have come close to your dream?
102. What have you done before that you can do again to move toward your future?
103. Who are people you trust and value who have supported you in the past and will again?
104. If you knew you couldn't fail, what would you do now?
105. What one thing could you do today that would take you nearer to your goal?
106. If you were the bravest version of yourself today, what would you be doing?
107. What will you do today to move you closer to your desired outcome?
108. Where is your life out of balance?
109. What is the legacy that you want to leave?
110. What vision do you have for yourself in the next year?
111. What are you willing to do in the next 30 days?
112. Who is someone that you know, or that you've heard of or read about, that you really admire?
113. What do you want to be doing in five years time?
114. What new skill do you want to learn or develop?
115. If you knew that this was your last year on the planet, what would you start doing you haven't been doing? What would you stop doing that you are currently doing?
116. How does this goal impact your spouse/partner?
117. What's the excuse that you have always used for not achieving your goals?
118. If you weren't holding anything back, what would you be doing?

119. What would your ideal daily schedule look like?
120. If you were happier, how would people know?
121. What are you unclear about in your life?
122. What have you been worried about lately? What's the truth?
123. Does your current habitat fully support who you're becoming?
124. Tell me how a person you admire would handle this situation.
125. Who wouldn't like it if you succeeded?
126. Will this choice move you forward or keep you stuck?
127. What will your impact be 100 years from now?
128. What's next for you?
129. Instead of either/or, how could you use both?
130. What rules do you have that are getting in the way?
131. If we meet three years from today, what has to have happened during that three-year period for you to feel happy about your progress?
132. What are the biggest dangers that you'll have to face and deal with in order to achieve that progress?
133. What are the biggest opportunities that you have that you would need to focus on and capture to achieve those things?
134. What strengths do you need to reinforce and maximize?
135. What skills and resources do you need to develop that you don't currently have in order to capture those opportunities?
136. What are you telling yourself about reaching your destination?
137. What story is holding you back?
138. Describe your three greatest accomplishments to date. What made these accomplishments stand out for you?
139. What gives you energy?
140. What are times you feel at your best?
141. What do you most value about yourself?
142. What do you want more of?
143. What worked well for you before? What's working well now?
144. What are you doing each day that's living your dream?
145. What does it feel like when you experience this level of success?
146. Where is your life out of balance?
147. Which relationships do you value the most? Why are they important to you?
148. What is your life's calling?
149. What's keeping you from pursuing your life's calling?

Business Coaching Questions

150. What would need to happen for you to walk away feeling that this was a success?
151. What would we need to change for this to become an opportunity, rather than a challenge?
152. Which of your strengths become a limitation when you exercise it too much?
153. Who do you need to add to the team to make this a success?
154. How committed do you feel to this goal?
155. If you could change one thing about the goal what would it be?
156. Which of your core values does this goal express?
157. How could you have this conversation so it empowers everyone involved?
158. How can you create more value with less effort?
159. How can you learn what you need to know about this?
160. Who else will benefit?
161. Do you have a detailed strategy to get there?
162. What can you do to expand your thinking?
163. What would you do if time was not an issue?
164. What are some options to consider?
165. What are the pros and cons of each option?
166. What resources do you have/need?
167. What specifically are you going to do next?
168. When are you going to do it?
169. What strengths will you draw on to help you?
170. How can you get the help/resources you need?
171. What do you need to ensure you move forward?

THE ULTIMATE GUIDE TO COACHING QUESTIONS

Career Coaching Questions

172. What career challenges excites you the most in your life right now?
173. When you were in college, what did you envision for yourself and for your career?
174. What excites you about the work you are doing?
175. How important is security to you?
176. When was the last time you did something that scared you?
177. What is your greatest career fear?
178. What is your number one confidence barrier?
179. Where do you do your best thinking?
180. What do you think your performance barriers are?
181. What does success mean to you?
182. What new behavior would help you achieve your goals?
183. If you could spend the rest of your life doing the most amazing thing you've ever dreamed of, what would you be doing?
184. What jobs would allow you to do the most amazing thing?
185. What obstacles stand in your way?
186. What life and professional experiences equip you for your next career?
187. What new experiences or skills might help you reach your career goals?
188. How could you leverage your network to find the best fit?
189. What's one small step you could take to explore the possibilities in this new industry?
190. What did you like about your prior job (where you stayed several years)? What kept you there?
191. What do you want to be doing 5 years from now?
192. What is most energizing about your work?
193. Why do you stay?
194. What might lure you away?
195. What are your top five strengths? How could you build on your strengths?
196. What strengths and talents would you like to carry into your future?
197. Where do you see yourself excelling?
198. What's your career vision and plan?
199. What things from your daily life make you happy?
200. What is your definition of success?

Now What?

From the 200 coaching questions above, create your own list of coaching questions. Select the questions that resonate with you and put them in a document. Print the document out and keep it in front of you at all times. Challenge yourself to incorporate at least three coaching questions in your daily conversations. From there, try different coaching models until you find a coaching model that speaks to you. Build your level of skill with that coaching model. Over time, assess how effective your ascribed coaching model is in helping your clients get the results they're looking for… and then repeat, repeat, repeat. As Don Miguel Ruiz has said, "Repetition makes the master." Mastery as a coach comes in one way and one way only: through practice.

CHAPTER 6: WHAT'S NEXT?

Don't ignore your own potential.
- Unknown

Developing your coaching skills is a lifelong process. As you develop as a person, you'll develop as a coach. As you connect with other coaches, work with different types of clients, and pursue additional coach training, you'll become a stronger coach. Remember that your strength as a coach is about living the mastery journey and not mastering the coaching process. The more you engage in the daily, deliberate learning and practice of coaching, the better you'll become as a coach.

The point is simple: to become a great coach, coach more. Coach outside of your comfort zone. Coach when you're not in the mood to coach. Coach when you don't feel perfect and life isn't calm. Coach under all circumstances and coach as soon as you can. Don't wait until you've gotten five coaching credentials, have worked for three years as a coach for someone else, and have at least two hundred clients under your belt. Your greatness as a coach isn't determined by a certain number of credentials or years. Every coaching moment gives you the opportunity to be great. Don't miss out because you don't feel ready. Your entire life will be spent pursuing coaching mastery.

And… start building your coaching business before you 'feel' ready. Read that again. One of the fastest ways to build your coaching practice comes through building an email list. I devoted an entire book to how do this in Email Marketing For Coaches. Do not second guess your ability to, on the one hand, move towards coaching mastery and, on the other hand, focus on coaching business success. You need to do BOTH and you have every ability to do BOTH at the same time. Check out Email Marketing For Coaches: How to Build Your Email List and Grow Your Coaching Business and start building your email list today…

At the end of the day, you'll become the coach you decide to become. It all begins with what you believe about you. Don't base your success on external validation. It won't last. As a coach, there will be lulls in your coaching practice. There will be droughts in your coaching business. There will be times when you take on resistant clients who are making no progress. None of that should define your mission or change what you believe about your work in the world.

Start today by believing in your ability to coach others. Continue tomorrow by practicing the coaching techniques shared in this book (and practice them consistently). Follow through by sharing your talents and gifts with the world. If no one knows about you, they have no opportunity to hire you as a coach. At the end of the day, the only person who can decide what kind of coach you'll become is you. Choose greatness now…

WOULD YOU LIKE TO KNOW MORE?

Seeing individuals step into their full power is one of my life purposes. I fulfill that mission in a number of ways and I invite you to join me on the journey.

Join me in Mindset Mastery for Coaches on Facebook!
Join a FREE private Facebook group where you'll have opportunities to connect with like-minded coaches. I also host a weekly live video coaching call where we'll discuss mindset, business building, and how to grow your coaching practice.

Enroll in my courses on Skillshare
I've created a number of courses that you can take on the Skillshare platform. Follow me on Skillshare by visiting https://www.skillshare.com/user/kassandravaughn.

She Runs The Show
If you're a woman entrepreneur, an aspiring entrepreneur, or have any female friends who are thinking about entrepreneurship, invite them to join the movement and visit my blog at http://www.sherunstheshow.com. I host monthly teleseminars, webinars, and offer online programs that help women take their businesses to the next level. I also host an iTunes podcast for She Runs the Show. You can find the latest episode at: http://tinyurl.com/sherunstheshowpodcast.

Looking for a speaker?

I love to facilitate workshops, lectures, and conference talks on the topics of focus, resiliency, grit, personal power, and self-worth. If you'd like to discuss my speaking at your event or creating a corporate workshop for your company, please contact me at info@kassandravaughn.com.

Check out my other books

I love to write about overcoming fear and developing focus. Feel free to check out my other books at www.overcomingfearbooks.com.

If you have any questions, comments, or feedback, please email me at info@kassandravaughn.com.
I'd love to hear from you!

DID YOU LIKE THE BOOK?

If you liked the book, please recommend the eBook to friends, family, and any person you know who needs to read this. Also, please leave a review on Amazon and let me know how you felt about the book and what the book was able to help you accomplish. I'm always checking the reviews.

I'd love to respond to you personally. After you've left your Amazon review, please email me at info@kassandravaughn.com to let me know. Thanks in advance!

Kassandra Vaughn

Printed in Great Britain
by Amazon